WACKY COMPARISONS
HOW TALL?

by Mark Weakland   illustrated by Igor Sinkovec

Wacky Ways to COMPARE HEIGHT

How tall is a PENGUIN?

How tall is a SKUNK?

Is either as tall as a TREE or CHIPMUNK?

A GIRAFFE, a DINO, a SOCCER BALL—

Time to discover how short and how tall!

PICTURE WINDOW BOOKS
a capstone imprint

21 SKUNKS, with a little luck, stand as tall as

1 GARBAGE TRUCK.

An **NBA PLAYER** with a basketball is almost as tall as **7** STYLISH DOLLS.

1 player = 6 ft., 8 in. (2 m); 1 doll = 1 ft. (30 cm)

470 CHATTERING CHIPMUNKS can be

1 TOWERING REDWOOD TREE.

as tall as

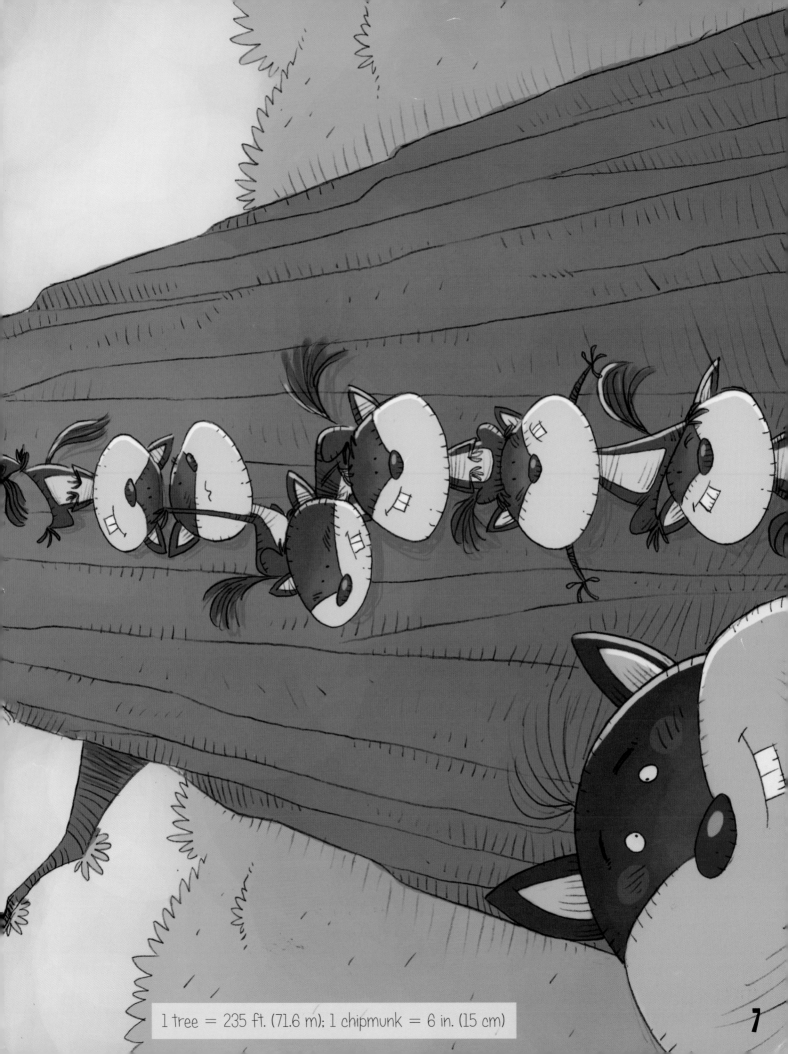

1 tree = 235 ft. (71.6 m); 1 chipmunk = 6 in. (15 cm)

To see to the top, we crane our necks.
36 HOT DOGS equal 1 T. REX!

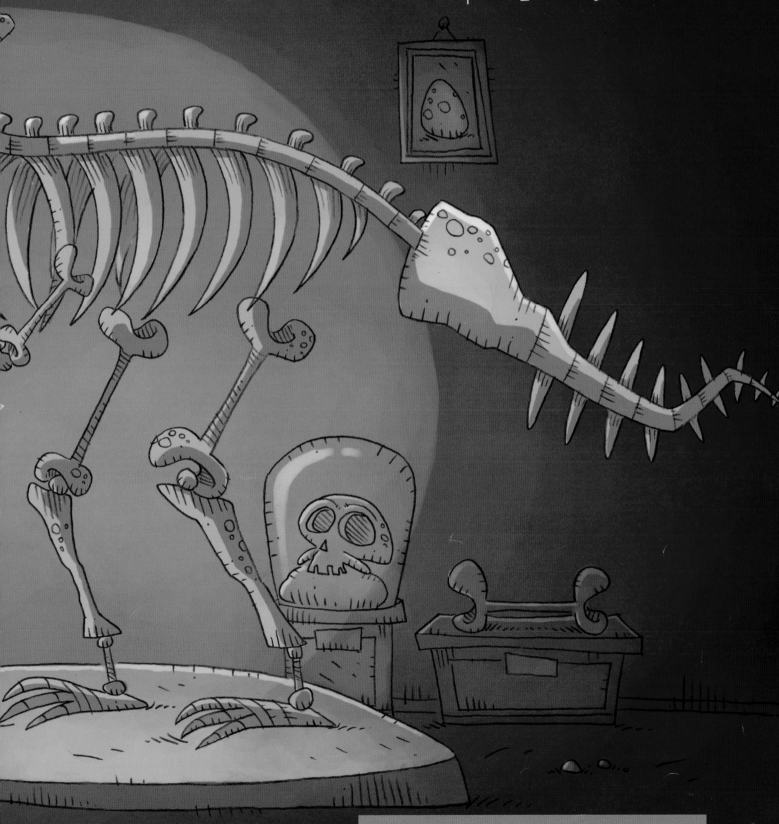

"The STATUE OF LIBERTY is tall. It's true!"

say **431** PIGEONS who wobble and coo.

1 statue = 305 ft. (93 m); 1 pigeon = 8½ in. (22 cm)

The GREAT PYRAMID has a height a bit greater than **84** REFRIGERATORS.

1 pyramid = 450 ft. (137 m); 1 fridge = 5 ft., 4 in. (1.6 m)

Just clearing the height
of **1 GIRAFFE,**

GIRAFFE

14 TEDDY BEARS

stand tall and laugh.

BEARS

1 giraffe = 17 ft. (5.2 m); 1 bear = 1 ft., 3 in. (38 cm)

1 OSTRICH, feathered and tall,

nearly equals the height of **11** SOCCER BALLS.

1 ostrich = 8 ft. (2.4 m); 1 ball = 9 in. (23 cm)

An ELEPHANT,

from bottom to top,

The world's tallest mountain is

MOUNT EVEREST.

How many ELEPHANTS match

its snowy crest?

2,765

1 mountain = 29,035 ft. (8.8 kilometers); 1 elephant = 10 ft. 6 in. (3.2 m)

How many **POPSICLES** should you buy

to match the height of a **BIRD** that can't fly?

Hope you enjoyed this book about height.

And now this penguin says, "Good night!"

READ MORE

Cleary, Brian P. *How Long or How Wide?: A Measuring Guide*. Math Is Categorical. Minneapolis: Millbrook Press, 2007.

Hillman, Ben. *How Big Is It?: A Big Book All About BIGness*. What's the Big Idea? New York: Scholastic Reference, 2007.

Parker, Vic. *How Tall Is Tall?: Comparing Structures*. Measuring and Comparing. Chicago: Heinemann Library, 2011.

INTERNET SITES

FactHound offers a safe, fun way to find Internet sites related to this book. All of the sites on FactHound have been researched by our staff.

Here's all you do:

Visit *www.facthound.com*

Type in this code: 9781404883239

Special thanks to our adviser, Terry Flaherty, PhD, Professor of English, Minnesota State University, Mankato, for his expertise.

Editor: Jill Kalz
Designer: Ashlee Suker
Art Director: Nathan Gassman
Production Specialist: Eric Manske
The illustrations in this book were created digitally.

Picture Window Books are published by Capstone,
1710 Roe Crest Drive, North Mankato, Minnesota 56003
www.capstonepub.com

Library of Congress Cataloging-in-Publication Data
Weakland, Mark.
  How tall? : wacky ways to compare height / by Mark Weakland ; illustrated by Igor Sinkovec.
      pages cm. — (Wacky comparisons)
  Summary: "Compares various tall objects to shorter objects in unique, illustrated ways"—Provided by publisher.
  Audience: K to grade 3.
  Includes bibliographical references.
  ISBN 978-1-4048-8323-9 (library binding)
  ISBN 978-1-4795-1913-2 (paperback)
  ISBN 978-1-4795-1909-5 (eBook PDF)
1. Measurement—Juvenile literature. 2. Comparison (Philosophy)—Juvenile literature. I. Sinkovec, Igor, illustrator. II. Title.

QA465.W43 2014
530.8—dc23   2013012150

Printed in the United States of America in North Mankato, Minnesota.
032013   007223CGF13

LOOK FOR ALL THE BOOKS IN THE SERIES:

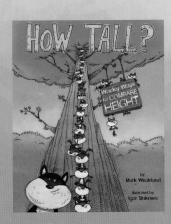